APHIC NOVELS

TEACHER'S GUI

VERSUS

SERIES

Contents

Introduction to Impact Graphic Novels ii
Overview of Versus series iv
Scope and Sequence of Skills v
Instructional Path. vii
Features of Impact Teacher's Guides viii

Lesson 1: Team Spirit Theme—Perseverance 2
- Literary Response Skill: Analyze Character
- Comprehension Skill: Determining Importance
- Literature Connection: *The Old Man and the Sea*, Ernest Hemingway; *Hatchet*, Gary Paulsen

Lesson 2: Home Troubles Theme—Respect. 8
- Literary Response Skill: Analyze Plot
- Comprehension Skill: Comparing and Contrasting
- Literature Connection: *To Kill a Mockingbird*, Harper Lee; *Freak the Mighty*, Rodman Philbrick

Lesson 3: Falling Apart Theme—Integrity. 14
- Literary Response Skill: Analyze Setting
- Comprehension Skill: Finding Cause and Effect
- Literature Connection: *Julius Caesar*, William Shakespeare; *Holes*, Louis Sachar

Lesson 4: In Other Hands Theme—Courage 20
- Literary Response Skill: Foreshadowing
- Comprehension Skill: Making Inferences
- Literature Connection: *The Red Badge of Courage*, Stephen Crane; *The Outsiders*, S. E. Hinton

Lesson 5: To the Wire Theme—Responsibility 26
- Literary Response Skill: Analyze Irony
- Comprehension Skill: Identifying Theme
- Literature Connection: *The Call of the Wild*, Jack London; *The Pigman*, Paul Zindel

Skill Masters

Literary Response

Character Traits Web 6
Story Sequence Chart. 12
Setting—Where and When . . 18
Foreshadowing. 24
Irony 30

Comprehension

Determining Importance 7
Compare and Contrast. 13
Cause and Effect 19
Making Inferences 25
What's the Theme?. 31
Writing Master. 32

Steck Vaughn™
A Harcourt Achieve Imprint
www.Steck-Vaughn.com
1-800-531-5015

Motivating Graphic Novels Build Better Readers and Citizens

Thrilling storylines that engage the most reluctant readers.

Fascinating cast of teen-aged characters.

Finally, books your students want to read—at a grade 3–5 readability!

"The graphic novel is being recognized for its contribution to the development of both visual and verbal literacy … to fully grasp the meaning of the story."

– Michelle Gorman, *Getting Graphic! Using Graphic Novels to Promote Literacy with Preteens and Teens*

mpact Graphic Novels or Your Struggling Readers

Readers can identify with the characters who overcome fears and insecurities, deal with family and social conflicts, and learn to contribute to those around them.

Your students will learn core character values as they're engaged in the high-interest, visually stimulating novels.

Watch as your struggling readers become motivated to thinking critically about a story as they practice key comprehension and literary response skills.

Impact Graphic Novels
look and read like the popular graphic novels in bookstores today!

Your students won't get enough of these exciting stories!

Three Exciting Series Reflect Issues That Impact Students' Everyday Lives

ORION

A secret task force of superpowered teens travel through space to save the world from alien invaders.

SHADOWCAST

A group of strangers are lost on a mysterious, deserted island and have to work together to find their way home.

VERSUS

This series of books follows a group of high school students touring the world in an international sports competition. The characters in *Versus* learn . . .

"When teachers bring to the fore the character dimension of the curriculum, they enhance the relevance of subject matter . . . and in the process, increase student engagement and achievement."

– Tom Lickona, *Eleven Principles of Effective Character Education*

'un Books, /aluable Skills Instruction

Versus Series Volumes	5 Themes	5 Literary Response Skills	5 Comprehension Skills
Team Spirit	Perseverance	Analyze Character	Determining Importance
Home Troubles	Respect	Analyze Plot	Comparing and Contrasting
Falling Apart	Integrity	Analyze Setting	Finding Cause and Effect
In Other Hands	Courage	Foreshadowing	Making Inferences
To the Wire	Responsibility	Analyze Irony	Identifying Theme

Connection to Grade-Level Literature Through Literary Themes

The five universal themes in each *Impact Graphic Novels* series connect to more complex literature. The teacher's guides offer suggested titles from core reading curriculum and examples of how to make the thematic connection.

These Stories Make a Positive Impact!

Your students will be motivated and inspired by what the *Impact* characters go through, the challenges they overcome, and the lessons they learn.

Perseverance
- *The Old Man and the Sea,* Ernest Hemingway
- *Hatchet,* Gary Paulsen

Respect
- *To Kill a Mockingbird,* Harper Lee
- *Freak the Mighty,* Rodman Philbrick

Integrity
- *Julius Caesar,* William Shakespeare
- *Holes,* Louis Sachar

Courage
- *The Red Badge of Courage,* Stephen Crane
- *The Outsiders,* S. E. Hinton

Responsibility
- *The Call of the Wild,* Jack London
- *The Pigman,* Paul Zindel

Clear Instruction With Meaningful Independent Work

Simple, easy-to-follow instruction and independent study opportunities make this reading series ideal for teachers, paraprofessionals, or volunteers.

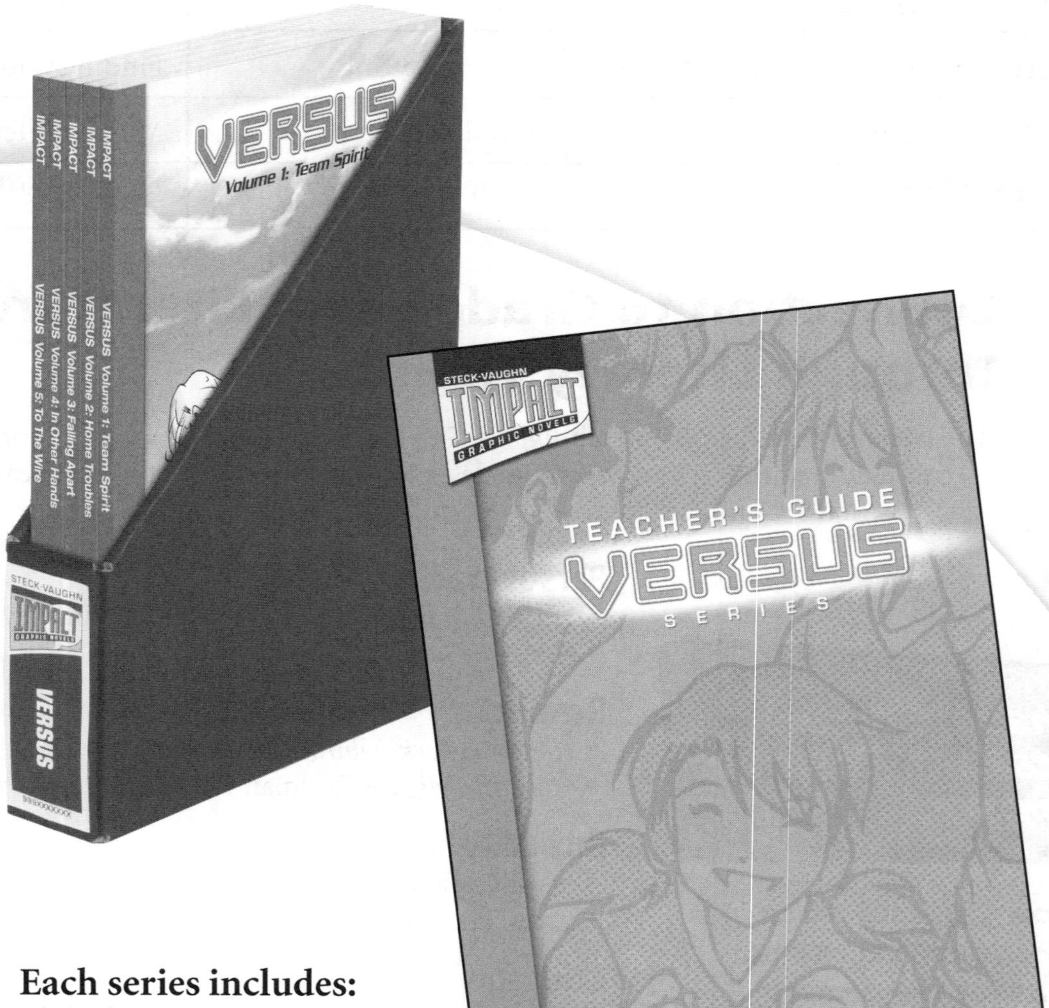

Each series includes:
- 5 student volumes
- 1 Teacher's Guide

Instructional Path

Set the Scene

Focus on Literary Response
Students learn and practice one key literary response skill.

Focus on Comprehension
Students learn and practice one key comprehension skill.

Review and Extend
Students review and practice both literary response and comprehension skills.

Wrap-Up

Each section has the same structure:

Teach Direct instruction and modeling of skills provides the foundation for learning.

Read Paired, silent reading time provides support for a variety of reading levels.

Discuss Student-focused, rich discussion motivates struggling readers to talk about the books.

Write Self-managed blackline masters connect independent work to each day's instruction.

Students learn literary response skills as they talk about the story.

Students connect personally to the theme, characters, and plot. Students also share what they know and like about graphic novels.

Each lesson provides an example of how to accommodate the teaching process for your English language learners.

Lesson 1

Versus *Volume 1*
Team Spirit

Summary: The top high school athletes from across the country have gathered in Washington, D.C. Only the best can join Team U.S.A. Tempers flare and spirits soar when we find out who goes home and who's made the cut!

Lesson Overview

Theme: Perseverance
Literary Response Skill: Analyze Character
Comprehension Skill: Determining Importance
Literature Connection: *The Old Man and the Sea,* by Ernest Hemingway; *Hatchet,* by Gary Paulsen

Before Reading

Set the Scene

Connect to Personal Experience

- Ask students to talk about a time when they had to work hard to achieve a goal.
- Have students give examples of athletes, musicians, and people they know who *persevered,* or kept trying in difficult times. Have them talk about other people who gave up.

Get Motivated

- Tell students that they will be reading about a group of characters who face struggles and sometimes want to give up.
- Distribute copies of *Team Spirit.* Turn to the inside front cover and go over the instructions for reading graphic novels. Have students look at the cover, skim the pages, and share their thoughts. Ask: *Have you ever read a graphic novel? What do you like about this book? How do you think it will be different from other books you have read in this class?*

About the Characters

- Turn to pp. 2–3. Have a volunteer read the summary (p. 3). Ask: *What do we know about the characters? What obstacles will they face in this book?*

2 IMPACT GRAPHIC NOVELS

During Reading

Focus on Literary Response: Analyze Character

Teach

- Explain that we *analyze characters* in novels through their speech, appearance, thoughts, actions, and what other characters think or say about them. Have students turn to pp. 2–3 in *Team Spirit* and comment on what they think the characters will be like based on their appearances.
- Read aloud Chapter 1, pp. 4–9. Model a think-aloud: *Aisha says, "Move over and let me have a better look!" I think she's pushy. I wonder if her pushy attitude will affect whether she makes the team.* Continue the discussion by asking students what they think of other characters with supporting evidence from the text.

Read

- Pair students of differing abilities to read the rest of Chapter 1. Have partners read four pages silently, signal to the other with a thumbs-up or other silent signal when they're done, and wait quietly for the other to finish. Then each should share a thought or question about a character. Continue in this way to the end of the chapter.

Discuss

- Ask questions to help students gain an understanding of the characters:

  After reading page 5, what do you think of Ron's attitude? Do you know anyone like Ron?

  What do you think is Ricardo's biggest obstacle? (p. 16)

  What struggles are Sammy and Dennis facing? (pp. 22–23) How would you handle the same situation?

Write

- Distribute **Skill Master 1: Character Traits Web** on p. 6. Students can work with their partners to complete the activity. Have students share elements of their completed webs.
- On a separate sheet of paper, ask students to choose their favorite character and write about why they chose that particular character. Have students explain whether the character turned out differently from their expectations.

Skill Master 1

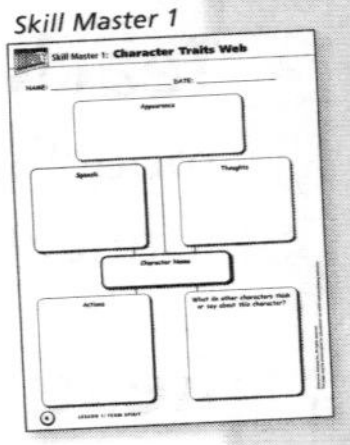

ELL Support for English Language Learners

Some students may be unfamiliar with basketball and softball. As they read about the characters on pp. 2–3 of *Team Spirit,* point to the equipment the characters are holding and explain these sports in more detail. Invite students to tell about sports that are common to their culture.

Focus on Comprehension: Determining Importance

Teach

- Explain that comprehending a story begins with understanding which events and details in the story are important. *Determining importance* helps the reader keep the story straight and anticipate what may happen next.
- Recount the plot of a familiar story or movie, overemphasizing minor characters, events, and details. Ask volunteers to retell the story, focusing this time on the important details and leaving out unimportant ones.

LESSON 1: TEAM SPIRIT 3

Rich discussions before, during, and after reading drive to a deeper understanding of the storyline and characters.

Students learn comprehension strategies as they talk about the story.

After each teaching moment, students have the opportunity to practice independently using blackline masters.

Each lesson provides an example of how to accommodate the teaching process for your students with special needs.

Support for **Students with Special Needs**

Once students determine important details in Chapter 1, provide them with sports articles from newspapers or magazines. Students should circle important details that help them determine the main idea of the articles.

Skill Master 2

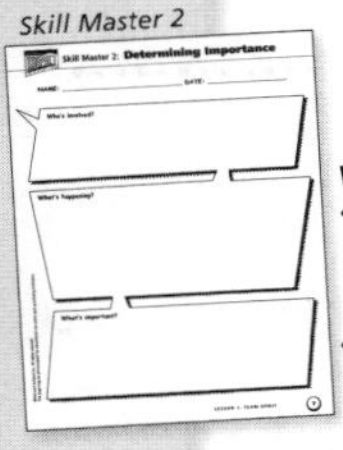

Read

- Have students briefly retell the key characters, events, and details of Chapter 1.
- Pair students of differing abilities to read Chapter 2, urging students to pay attention to important events and details. Have partners read four pages silently, signal to the other with a thumbs-up or other silent signal when they're done, and wait quietly for the other to finish. Then each should share a thought or question that comes up while reading. Continue in this way to the end of the chapter.

Discuss

- Ask students questions to help them determine important events and details in Chapter 2:

  What is bothering Cindy? When do we find out about her problem? (p. 37) How would you deal with this situation?

  What is Coach Jerry's secret? When do we find this out? (p. 43) Do you think he should continue with the competition?

  How does Aisha react when Ron suggests that they "help each other" look good during the matches? (pp. 38–39) What do you think about Aisha now?

Write

- Distribute **Skill Master 2: Determining Importance** on p. 7. Have partners complete the activity by filling in information from Chapter 2. Ask volunteers to share elements of their completed activity. Have students settle any questions regarding importance of events or details by referring to the text.
- On a separate sheet of paper, ask students to describe briefly the key events in their favorite book, story, television program, or movie. Remind them to write these events in the correct order.

Review and Extend

Teach

- **Analyze Character** Remind students that characters are described through their speech, appearance, thoughts, actions, and what other characters think or say about them. Help students remember each character's traits and the problems they face.
- **Determining Importance** Remind students that determining important events and details in the story helps us understand what the story is about. Remembering the order in which these things happen can give us clues about what may happen next. Ask a volunteer to recall what happened in Chapter 2. Have other students assist in order to recount key events in the proper order.

Read

- Have students briefly retell the key events and details of Chapter 2.
- Pair students of differing abilities to read Chapter 3. Ask students to remember to pay attention to character traits and the key events. Have partners read four pages silently, signal to the other with a thumbs-up or other silent signal when they're done, and wait quietly for the other to finish. Then each should share a thought or question about how a character's personality is important to the story. Continue in this way to the end of the chapter.

Discuss

- Ask questions to help students gain an understanding of the characters' traits and the important events in Chapter 3:

  How did Ricardo's perseverance throughout the story help the Eagles become Team U.S.A.? (Ricardo inspired his teammates by practicing, staying positive, and being a team player.)

  How did Maggie's and Ron's traits help determine the key events in the story? (Maggie helped Ron show off because she thought he liked her.)

  If Ron hadn't been so selfish, what do you think would have happened differently in the story?

Writing Master

Write

- Distribute copies of the **Writing Master** on p. 40. Ask students to choose one character who really had to persevere in the story and describe the key events that show the character's perseverance. Have students tell how the character's traits help or hinder the character in reaching his or her goals.

After Reading

Wrap-Up

Discuss

- Allow students to reflect on what they have read.

  Which character would you most like to have as a friend? Why?

  Do you know anybody like Maggie, Ron, or Ricardo?

  Do any of the characters remind you of yourself? Of someone you know?

  How could each character change in order to make the team stronger?

  Have you ever had to change for the good of a team?

Connect to Literature

Connect the theme of perseverance to classroom literature, such as Hemingway's *The Old Man and the Sea* or Paulsen's *Hatchet*. For example:

- *Santiago, in* The Old Man and the Sea, *fights for three days to catch the huge marlin, even when sharks attack. Santiago shows perseverance. What character in* Team Spirit *shows perseverance? How are the situations alike and different?*
- *In* Hatchet, *after Brian is attacked by the porcupine, he mopes in his shelter. Then he resolves to persevere by making the best of things. This attitude gets him through the moose attack and the tornado. Can you think of a part in* Team Spirit *similar to this? How is it different?*

Relates the literary response skill to the comprehension skill, using the lesson theme.

Discussions are framed around students' personal response to the characters. This springboards into discussion about a similar theme in a **grade-level literary selection.**

Lesson 1

Versus *Volume 1*
Team Spirit

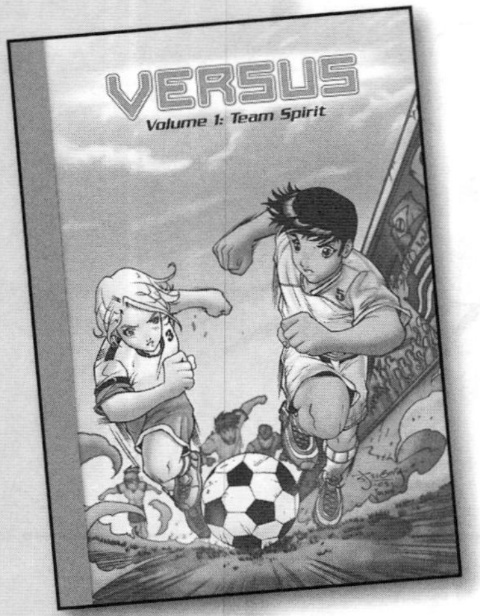

Summary: The top high school athletes from across the country have gathered in Washington, D.C. Only the best can join Team U.S.A. Tempers flare and spirits soar when we find out who goes home and who's made the cut!

Lesson Overview

Theme: Perseverance

Literary Response Skill: Analyze Character

Comprehension Skill: Determining Importance

Literature Connection: *The Old Man and the Sea,* by Ernest Hemingway; *Hatchet,* by Gary Paulsen

Before Reading

Set the Scene

Connect to Personal Experience

- Ask students to talk about a time when they had to work hard to achieve a goal.
- Have students give examples of athletes, musicians, and people they know who *persevered,* or kept trying in difficult times. Have them talk about other people who gave up.

Get Motivated

- Tell students that they will be reading about a group of characters who face struggles and sometimes want to give up.
- Distribute copies of *Team Spirit.* Turn to the inside front cover and go over the instructions for reading graphic novels. Have students look at the cover, skim the pages, and share their thoughts. Ask: *Have you ever read a graphic novel? What do you like about this book? How do you think it will be different from other books you have read in this class?*

About the Characters

- Turn to pp. 2–3. Have a volunteer read the summary (p. 3). Ask: *What do we know about the characters? What obstacles will they face in this book?*

During Reading

Focus on Literary Response: Analyze Character

Teach

- Explain that we *analyze characters* in novels through their speech, appearance, thoughts, actions, and what other characters think or say about them. Have students turn to pp. 2–3 in *Team Spirit* and comment on what they think the characters will be like based on their appearances.
- Read aloud Chapter 1, pp. 4–9. Model a think-aloud: *Aisha says, "Move over and let me have a better look!" I think she's pushy. I wonder if her pushy attitude will affect whether she makes the team.* Continue the discussion by asking students what they think of other characters with supporting evidence from the text.

Read

- Pair students of differing abilities to read the rest of Chapter 1. Have partners read four pages silently, signal to the other with a thumbs-up or other silent signal when they're done, and wait quietly for the other to finish. Then each should share a thought or question about a character. Continue in this way to the end of the chapter.

Discuss

- Ask questions to help students gain an understanding of the characters:

  After reading page 5, what do you think of Ron's attitude? Do you know anyone like Ron?

  What do you think is Ricardo's biggest obstacle? (p. 16)

  What struggles are Sammy and Dennis facing? (pp. 22–23) How would you handle the same situation?

Write

- Distribute **Skill Master 1: Character Traits Web** on p. 6. Students can work with their partners to complete the activity. Have students share elements of their completed webs.
- On a separate sheet of paper, ask students to choose their favorite character and write about why they chose that particular character. Have students explain whether the character turned out differently from their expectations.

Skill Master 1

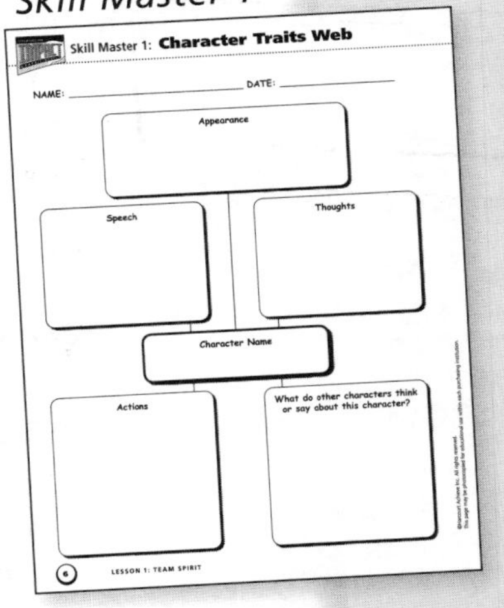
Skill Master 1: **Character Traits Web**

NAME: ____ DATE: ____

Appearance

Speech

Thoughts

Character Name

Actions

What do other characters think or say about this character?

6 LESSON 1: TEAM SPIRIT

ELL Support for English Language Learners

Some students may be unfamiliar with basketball and softball. As they read about the characters on pp. 2–3 of *Team Spirit*, point to the equipment the characters are holding and explain these sports in more detail. Invite students to tell about sports that are common to their culture.

Focus on Comprehension: Determining Importance

Teach

- Explain that comprehending a story begins with understanding which events and details in the story are important. *Determining importance* helps the reader keep the story straight and anticipate what may happen next.
- Recount the plot of a familiar story or movie, overemphasizing minor characters, events, and details. Ask volunteers to retell the story, focusing this time on the important details and leaving out unimportant ones.

Support for **Students with Special Needs**

Once students determine important details in Chapter 1, provide them with sports articles from newspapers or magazines. Students should circle important details that help them determine the main idea of the articles.

Skill Master 2

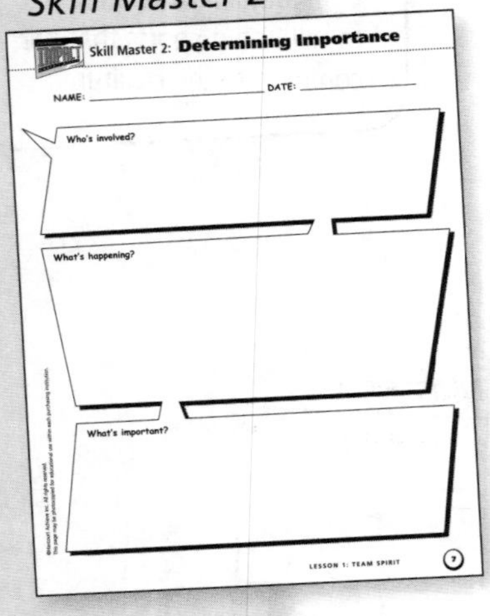
Skill Master 2: **Determining Importance**

NAME: ______ DATE: ______

Who's involved?

What's happening?

What's important?

LESSON 1: TEAM SPIRIT 7

Read

- Have students briefly retell the key characters, events, and details of Chapter 1.
- Pair students of differing abilities to read Chapter 2, urging students to pay attention to important events and details. Have partners read four pages silently, signal to the other with a thumbs-up or other silent signal when they're done, and wait quietly for the other to finish. Then each should share a thought or question that comes up while reading. Continue in this way to the end of the chapter.

Discuss

- Ask students questions to help them determine important events and details in Chapter 2:

  What is bothering Cindy? When do we find out about her problem? (p. 37) How would you deal with this situation?

  What is Coach Jerry's secret? When do we find this out? (p. 43) Do you think he should continue with the competition?

  How does Aisha react when Ron suggests that they "help each other" look good during the matches? (pp. 38–39) What do you think about Aisha now?

Write

- Distribute **Skill Master 2: Determining Importance** on p. 7. Have partners complete the activity by filling in information from Chapter 2. Ask volunteers to share elements of their completed activity. Have students settle any questions regarding importance of events or details by referring to the text.
- On a separate sheet of paper, ask students to describe briefly the key events in their favorite book, story, television program, or movie. Remind them to write these events in the correct order.

Review and Extend

Teach

- **Analyze Character** Remind students that characters are described through their speech, appearance, thoughts, actions, and what other characters think or say about them. Help students remember each character's traits and the problems they face.
- **Determining Importance** Remind students that determining important events and details in the story helps us understand what the story is about. Remembering the order in which these things happen can give us clues about what may happen next. Ask a volunteer to recall what happened in Chapter 2. Have other students assist in order to recount key events in the proper order.

Read

- Have students briefly retell the key events and details of Chapter 2.
- Pair students of differing abilities to read Chapter 3. Ask students to remember to pay attention to character traits and the key events. Have partners read four pages silently, signal to the other with a thumbs-up or other silent signal when they're done, and wait quietly for the other to finish. Then each should share a thought or question about how a character's personality is important to the story. Continue in this way to the end of the chapter.

Discuss

- Ask questions to help students gain an understanding of the characters' traits and the important events in Chapter 3:

  How did Ricardo's perseverance throughout the story help the Eagles become Team U.S.A.? (Ricardo inspired his teammates by practicing, staying positive, and being a team player.)

  How did Maggie's and Ron's traits help determine the key events in the story? (Maggie helped Ron show off because she thought he liked her.)

  If Ron hadn't been so selfish, what do you think would have happened differently in the story?

Write

- Distribute copies of the **Writing Master** on p. 40. Ask students to choose one character who really had to persevere in the story and describe the key events that show the character's perseverance. Have students tell how the character's traits help or hinder the character in reaching his or her goals.

Writing Master

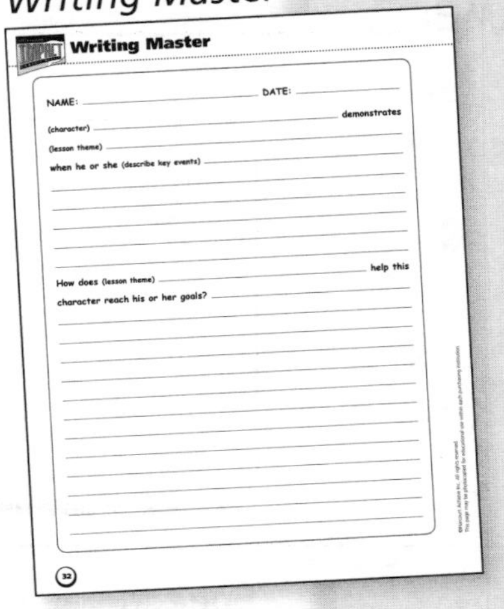
Writing Master

NAME: ______ DATE: ______

(character) ______ demonstrates

(lesson theme) ______

when he or she (describe key events) ______

How does (lesson theme) ______ help this

character reach his or her goals? ______

After Reading

Wrap-Up

Discuss

- Allow students to reflect on what they have read.

  Which character would you most like to have as a friend? Why?

  Do you know anybody like Maggie, Ron, or Ricardo?

  Do any of the characters remind you of yourself? Of someone you know?

  How could each character change in order to make the team stronger?

  Have you ever had to change for the good of a team?

Connect to Literature

Connect the theme of perseverance to classroom literature, such as Hemingway's *The Old Man and the Sea* or Paulsen's *Hatchet*. For example:

- *Santiago, in* The Old Man and the Sea, *fights for three days to catch the huge marlin, even when sharks attack. Santiago shows perseverance. What character in* Team Spirit *shows perseverance? How are the situations alike and different?*
- *In* Hatchet, *after Brian is attacked by the porcupine, he mopes in his shelter. Then he resolves to persevere by making the best of things. This attitude gets him through the moose attack and the tornado. Can you think of a part in* Team Spirit *similar to this? How is it different?*

STECK-VAUGHN IMPACT GRAPHIC NOVELS

Skill Master 1: **Character Traits Web**

NAME: ______________________________ DATE: ______________________

Appearance

Speech

Thoughts

Character Name

Actions

What do other characters think or say about this character?

Skill Master 2: **Determining Importance**

NAME: ______________________ DATE: ______________________

Who's involved?

What's happening?

What's important?

Versus *Volume 2*
Home Troubles

Summary: Team U.S.A. is up against some of the best teams in the International High School Sports Challenge. But Cindy is distracted by problems at home, and Ron is only interested in himself. Can the team pull together to win in South America?

Lesson Overview

Theme: Respect

Literary Response Skill: Analyze Plot

Comprehension Skill: Comparing and Contrasting

Literature Connection: *To Kill a Mockingbird,* by Harper Lee; *Freak the Mighty,* by Rodman Philbrick

Before Reading

Set the Scene

Connect to Personal Experience

- Ask students to talk about a recent time they felt appreciated and honored.
- Have them give examples of famous people or people they know whom they *respect,* or look up to. Ask: *Which qualities do you admire in these people?*

Get Motivated

- Tell students that they will continue reading about the athletes competing in the International High School Sports Challenge. As the athletes face challenges, both on and off the field, some try to pull the team together. Others are just out for themselves.
- Distribute copies of *Home Troubles.* Have students look at the cover, skim the pages, and share what they think will happen to the members of Team U.S.A.

About the Characters

- Ask students to turn to pp. 2–3. Allow a volunteer to read the summary (p. 3). Ask: *Which players do you think are most likely to have problems respecting others? How do you think that might affect the whole team?*

During Reading

Focus on Literary Response: Analyze Plot

Teach

- The *plot* is the series of related events that make up a story. Plot answers the question: *What happens?* It usually starts with a conflict, or problem. It also includes a climax, the most exciting part of a story as characters try to solve the conflict. The resolution is when the problem is solved and the story ends.
- Read aloud Chapter 1, pp. 4–9. Model a think-aloud: *Cindy is troubled but won't tell Maggie what's wrong. If Cindy's not focused, she could let the team down in competitions.* Continue the discussion about how Cindy's problems could affect the overall plot.

Read

- Pair students of differing abilities to read the rest of Chapter 1. Have partners read four pages silently, signal to the other with a thumbs-up or other silent signal when they're done, and wait quietly for the other to finish. Then each partner shares a thought about the most important events in the story so far. Continue in this way to the end of the chapter.

Discuss

- Lead students to a better understanding of the plot in Chapter 1:

  Why do the players begin to lose respect for Cindy? (p. 10)

  Why does Maggie seem conflicted about Ron? (p. 22) What does this scene tell you about both Maggie and Ron?

  At the end of the chapter, what is Coach Wagner struggling with? (p. 23) How would you feel if you found this out about your coach?

Write

- Distribute **Skill Master 3: Story Sequence Chart** on p. 12. Students should work with partners to complete the chart based on Chapter 1. They will continue the chart on their own after reading Chapters 2 and 3.
- On a separate sheet of paper, have students write a brief prediction of what will happen in the rest of *Home Troubles*. Remind them to include complications, a climax, and a resolution in their versions of the plot. Students may use their Story Sequence Chart as a reference.

ELL Support for English Language Learners

Some students may be unfamiliar with the rules of the games played in *Home Troubles*. Discuss what is going on during a sports scene. Focus on the rules of the games.

Skill Master 3

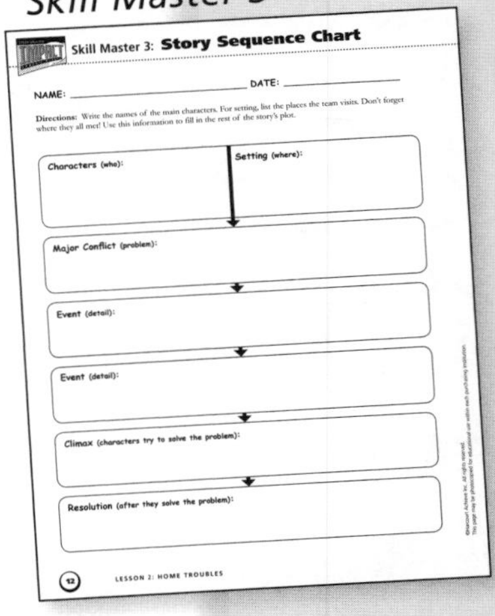

Focus on Comprehension: Comparing and Contrasting

Teach

- Explain that when we *compare* two or more things such as characters or events, we look at how they are similar. When we *contrast* two or more elements in a story, we look at how they are different.
- Compare and contrast two well-known actors, athletes, or singers. Draw a Venn diagram on the board and label each circle with a celebrity's name. Ask students to think of characteristics of each celebrity and have a volunteer record these in the circles. Any shared characteristics should be listed in the overlapping section.

Support for **Students with Special Needs**

As students read Chapter 2, show them how to make notes about two characters whom they will later compare and contrast. Have students make two columns and list characteristics as they read.

Skill Master 4

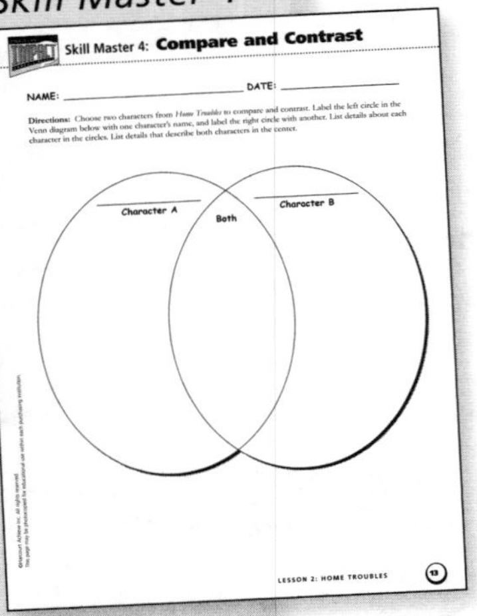
Skill Master 4: **Compare and Contrast**

NAME: ______________________ DATE: ______________

Directions: Choose two characters from *Home Troubles* to compare and contrast. Label the left circle in the Venn diagram below with one character's name, and label the right circle with another. List details about each character in the circles. List details that describe both characters in the center.

Read

- Ask a volunteer to recall what happens in Chapter 1.
- Pair students of differing abilities to read Chapter 2. Ask them to focus on two characters. Have partners read four pages silently, signal to the other with a thumbs-up or other silent signal when they're done, and wait quietly for the other to finish. Then each partner shares a thought about the two characters they chose—how they are alike and different. Students continue in this way to the end of the chapter.

Discuss

- Ask questions to help students gain an understanding of characters' similarities and differences:

  Compare Ron and Tony, a player from Team U.K. How are they alike? (p. 27) Have you competed against someone like Ron or Tony?

  Name one challenge that Team U.S.A. faces in this chapter. Have you experienced something similar? Explain.

Write

- Distribute **Skill Master 4: Compare and Contrast** on p. 13. Have students fill in each field of the Venn diagram with details from Chapter 2. Ask volunteers to share elements of their completed diagrams.
- On a separate sheet of paper, have students write two brief paragraphs comparing and contrasting two famous people. Encourage them to use a Venn diagram to organize their ideas before writing.

Review and Extend

Teach

- **Analyze Plot** Remind students that the events in a story make up the plot. The plot includes a conflict that is resolved by the end of the story. Ask students to remember the main events that make up the plot so far: *What are the problems that Cindy and Coach Wagner face in Chapters 1 and 2? Which problems are resolved in Chapter 2? Which are not?* Students may refer to their Story Sequence Charts.
- **Comparing and Contrasting** Remind students that comparing and contrasting involves finding similarities and differences. Draw a T-chart graphic organizer on the board. Write *respect* on one side and *disrespect* on the other. Have students raise their hands to suggest characters who belong in either category. Then ask volunteers to pick a character from each side and explain why each belongs on that side.

Read

- Ask a volunteer to recall what happens in Chapter 2.
- Pair students of differing abilities to read Chapter 3. Remind them to keep two characters in mind. Have partners read four pages silently, signal to the other with a thumbs-up or other silent signal when they're done, and wait quietly for the other to finish. Then each partner shares a thought about the two characters and how their actions affect the plot. Students continue in this way to the end of the chapter.

Discuss

- Lead students in a discussion about the plot and characters' similarities and differences. Ask questions that help students understand how respect or disrespect can affect the outcome of any conflict:

  How do Cindy's teammates help her resolve her family concerns and confidence problems? (pp. 59–61)

  Which character do you think is the most different from Ron? (Ricardo, Cindy) *How are you similar to or different from Ron?*

  How do the players' attitudes toward each other change from Chapter 1 to Chapter 3? (Most team members have begun to trust and respect each other, except for Ron.)

Writing Master

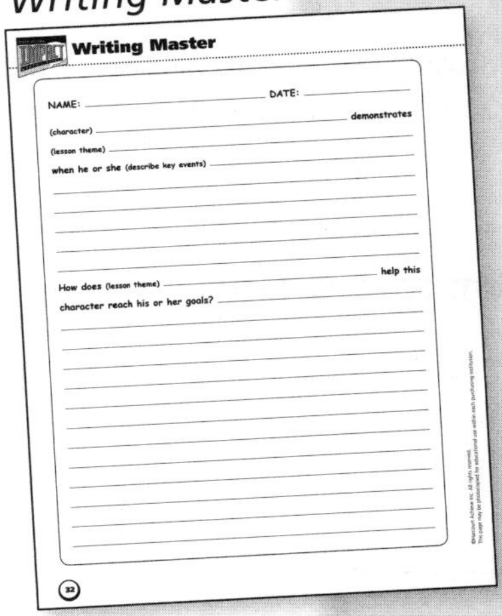
Writing Master

NAME: DATE:

(character) demonstrates

(lesson theme)

when he or she (describe key events)

How does (lesson theme) help this

character reach his or her goals?

Write

- Allow students to pair up to add information from Chapters 2 and 3 to their Story Sequence Charts.
- Distribute copies of the **Writing Master** on p. 40. Ask students to choose one character who demonstrates respect for the others. Have students discuss how this character's attitude affects the overall plot. Students should support their ideas with details from the selection.

After Reading

Wrap-Up

Discuss

- Allow students to reflect on what they have read.

  If you were on Team U.S.A., which teammate would you trust the most? Why?

  How might you have handled the situation if you were Ron? Maggie?

  How did you feel about Cindy at the beginning of the book? Did you respect her more at the end of the book? Why or why not?

Connect to Literature

Connect the theme of respect to classroom literature, such as Lee's *To Kill a Mockingbird* or Philbrick's *Freak the Mighty*. For example:

- *Atticus, in* To Kill a Mockingbird, *is respected in the town of Maycomb. People admire him because he treats others with respect, regardless of how much money they have or the color of their skin. Name a character in* Home Troubles *who reminds you of Atticus. In what ways are the two characters different?*
- *Max, the unlikely hero of Philbrick's* Freak the Mighty, *never fits in, mostly because others label him "learning disabled." Through a series of life-changing events, Max learns to respect himself. Cindy in* Home Troubles *is seen as a spoiled, rich girl. The others don't respect her, so she begins to doubt herself. How is this similar to and different from Max's story?*

Skill Master 3: **Story Sequence Chart**

NAME: ______________________________ DATE: ____________________

Directions: Write the names of the main characters. For setting, list the places the team visits. Don't forget where they all met! Use this information to fill in the rest of the story's plot.

Characters (who):

Setting (where):

Major Conflict (problem):

Event (detail):

Event (detail):

Climax (characters try to solve the problem):

Resolution (after they solve the problem):

Skill Master 4: **Compare and Contrast**

NAME: ______________________________ **DATE:** ____________________

Directions: Choose two characters from *Home Troubles* to compare and contrast. Label the left circle in the Venn diagram below with one character's name, and label the right circle with another. List details about each character in the circles. List details that describe both characters in the center.

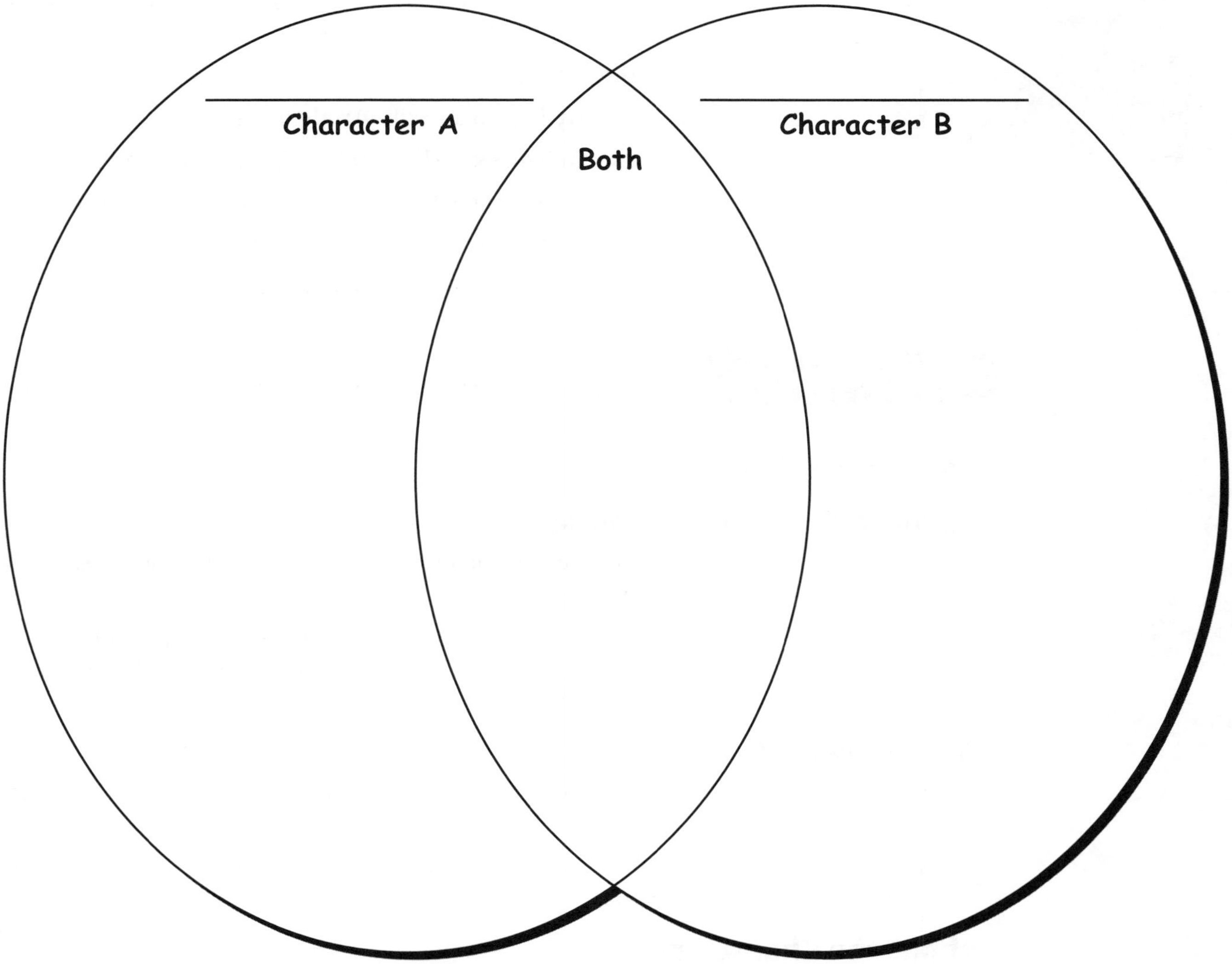

Lesson 3

Versus *Volume 3*
Falling Apart

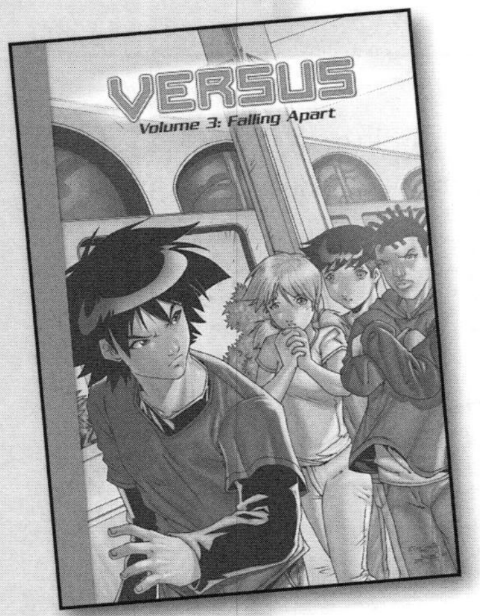

Summary: Team U.S.A. faces off against the famous Russian team in Moscow. Follow the members of Team U.S.A. as they struggle to band together and win another round of the tournament against all odds.

Lesson Overview

Theme: Integrity

Literary Response Skill: Analyze Setting

Comprehension Skill: Finding Cause and Effect

Literature Connection: *Julius Caesar,* by William Shakespeare; *Holes,* by Louis Sachar

Before Reading

Set the Scene

Connect to Personal Experience

- Ask students to talk about a time when someone surprised them with their honesty when it might have been easier just to lie.
- Ask students to think of examples of athletes, performers, politicians, or people they know who acted with *integrity,* or did the right thing when it wasn't easy to do. Discuss why we respect such people and their actions.

Get Motivated

- Tell students that in this volume, some members of Team U.S.A. face the challenge of doing the right thing.
- Distribute copies of *Falling Apart.* Have students look at the cover, skim the pages, and share what they think will happen to the members of Team U.S.A.

About the Characters

- Call students' attention to the title of the book, *Falling Apart.* Turn to pp. 2–3. Have a volunteer read the summary (p. 3). Model a think-aloud: *Things are starting to fall apart for Team U.S.A. Certain members of the team will have to wrestle with issues of personal integrity. Which members of the team do you think will be the most honest and trustworthy? What obstacles do you think they will face in this book?*

During Reading

Focus on Literary Response: Analyze Setting

Teach

- Explain that the *setting* of a story is the time and place in which the story happens. The setting creates the mood of the story. In graphic novels, the setting is described in pictures and words.
- Read aloud Chapter 1, pp. 4–10. Model a think-aloud: *As the team travels to Russia, Ron is planning how to become rich and famous. The mood in this part of the book is tense. I wonder whether Ron will be able to pressure others into letting him be the star of the team.*

Read

- Pair students of differing abilities to read the rest of Chapter 1. Have partners read four pages silently, signal to the other with a thumbs-up or other silent signal when they're done, and wait quietly for the other to finish. Then each partner shares a thought about the setting. Continue in this way to the end of the chapter.

Discuss

- Ask questions to help students understand how the setting affects the story:

  Look at the setting in which Ron and Maggie talk on pages 9–10. Do you think Maggie will help Ron? Why?

  What mood or atmosphere does the setting create when the criminals confront Aisha in her room? (p. 6) How do you think Aisha will handle her problem?

Write

- Distribute **Skill Master 5: Setting—Where and When** on p. 18. Partners should use details from Chapter 1 to complete the chart. They can continue the chart on their own after reading Chapters 2 and 3. Have them share details from their completed charts.
- Have students choose a scene from a book, movie, or TV show. On a separate sheet of paper, students should change the setting and rewrite the scene.

ELL Support for English Language Learners

Before reading *Falling Apart*, continue to discuss the theme of integrity with students who may need extra time to understand the term. Ask students to describe an important citizen, athlete, or politician from their culture who stood up for what was right, even though it meant trouble for them.

Skill Master 5

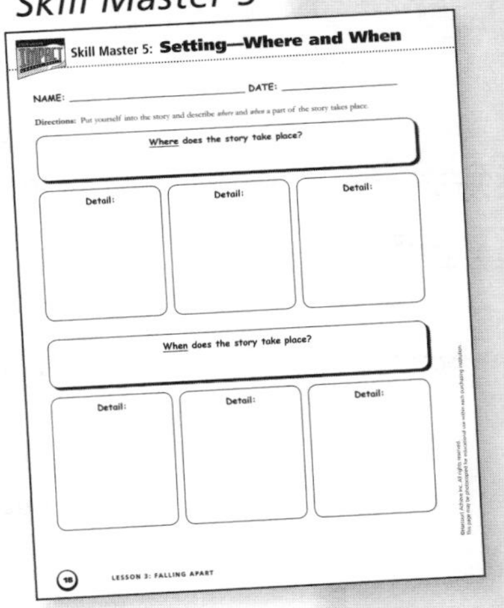
Skill Master 5: **Setting—Where and When**

NAME: ______ DATE: ______

Where does the story take place?

Detail: | Detail: | Detail:

When does the story take place?

Detail: | Detail: | Detail:

18 LESSON 3: FALLING APART

Focus on Comprehension: Finding Cause and Effect

Teach

- When we look for the *effect,* we are looking for "what happens." The *cause* is "why it happens."
- Pick a recent major event, such as a natural disaster, and discuss the chain of events leading to the big event. Identify what happened, why, and the results. It may help to create a flowchart on the board to help students follow the chain of causes and effects.

Support for **Students with Special Needs**

Instead of writing, allow students to find and cut out "before and after" pictures from magazines (e.g., advertisements for plant growth or hair restorers, natural disasters, construction). Students can paste pictures on chart paper, creating a pictorial cause and effect chart with arrows.

Skill Master 6

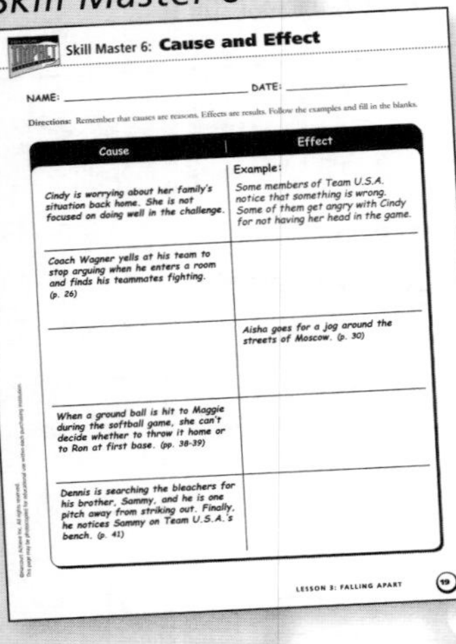

Skill Master 6: **Cause and Effect**

NAME: ______________________ DATE: ____________

Directions: Remember that causes are reasons. Effects are results. Follow the examples and fill in the blanks.

Cause	Effect
Cindy is worrying about her family's situation back home. She is not focused on doing well in the challenge.	Example: *Some members of Team U.S.A. notice that something is wrong. Some of them get angry with Cindy for not having her head in the game.*
Coach Wagner yells at his team to stop arguing when he enters a room and finds his teammates fighting. (p. 26)	
	Aisha goes for a jog around the streets of Moscow. (p. 30)
When a ground ball is hit to Maggie during the softball game, she can't decide whether to throw it home or to Ron at first base. (pp. 38-39)	
Dennis is searching the bleachers for his brother, Sammy, and he is one pitch away from striking out. Finally, he notices Sammy on Team U.S.A.'s bench. (p. 41)	

LESSON 3: FALLING APART 19

Read

- Have students summarize what happens in Chapter 1 of *Falling Apart.*
- Pair students of differing abilities to read Chapter 2, urging students to pay particular attention to the causes and effects of events while they read. Have partners read four pages silently, signal to the other with a thumbs-up or other silent signal when they're done, and wait quietly for the other to finish. Then each partner shares a thought about a cause or an effect. Continue in this way to the end of the chapter.

Discuss

- Guide students to find causes and effects in Chapter 2:

  What causes Ron to be mad at Maggie? (p. 24) How do Dennis, Aisha, and Cindy react to this? (pp. 25–26)

  Jerry is losing his patience with the whole team. Why? (pp. 25–27) How would you act in his place?

  Why do you think Jerry worries about the team's future if he is unable to continue coaching? Should he worry?

Write

- Distribute **Skill Master 6: Cause and Effect** on p. 19. Have partners complete the cause and effect chart with events from Chapter 2. Ask students to share information from their completed charts.
- On a separate sheet of paper, ask students to write about the causes and effects of an event from their own lives. What are some things they did that caused things to turn out a certain way? Students can use Skill Master 6 to help them organize their thoughts before writing.

Review and Extend

Teach

- **Analyze Setting** Remind students that setting refers to where and when a story takes place. Help students remember how setting is used in *Falling Apart* to create a mood or atmosphere, such as the hotel ballroom after Team U.S.A. lost to the Russian soccer team (p. 24).
- **Finding Cause and Effect** Remind students that effect is what happens and cause is why it happens. Ask a volunteer to recall important events in Chapter 2. Have other students identify the causes and effects of each event.

Read

- Have students summarize what happens in Chapters 1 and 2.
- Pair students of differing abilities to read Chapter 3. Have partners read four pages silently, signal to the other with a thumbs-up or other silent signal when they're done, and wait quietly for the other to finish. Then each partner shares a thought about what they read. Continue in this way to the end of the chapter.

Discuss

- Ask questions to help students understand setting and cause and effect:

  Falling Apart *is set in Russia. Do you think it makes a difference that the team is having to work through their problems far from home in a strange place?*

  By the end of the story, all of the members of Team U.S.A. are angry with Ron. What causes them to get to that point? (pp. 52–53)

  What would you do if you had a teammate like Ron?

Write

- Distribute copies of the **Writing Master** on p. 40. Ask students to choose one character who demonstrates integrity or a lack of integrity and analyze that character. Students should consider the causes and effects of the character's behavior, using examples from the book to support their ideas.

Writing Master

Writing Master

NAME: ____ DATE: ____

(character) ____ demonstrates

(lesson theme) ____

when he or she (describe key events) ____

How does (lesson theme) ____ help this

character reach his or her goals? ____

After Reading

Wrap-Up

Discuss

Allow students to reflect on what they have read.

Which character do you like the least? Why?

Which of the characters' actions are surprising?

Which character would you invite to meet your family or someone else important to you? Why?

Which character has the toughest decisions to make in the book?

Connect to Literature

Connect the theme of integrity to classroom literature, such as Shakespeare's *Julius Caesar* or Sachar's *Holes*. For example:

- *In Shakespeare's* Julius Caesar, *some people try to convince Brutus to help them in a plan to kill Caesar and take over the empire. At first, Brutus refuses to help them. How are the criminals in* Falling Apart *similar to the characters who try to take over in* Julius Caesar? *In what ways is Aisha like Brutus?*
- *In the book* Holes *by Louis Sachar, Stanley Yelnats shows integrity in the way he treats Zero, the least popular inmate of Camp Green Lake, even though others make fun of him. How does Ricardo in* Falling Apart *remind you of Stanley? How is Cindy in* Falling Apart *similar to Zero?*

Skill Master 5: **Setting—Where and When**

NAME: ______________________________ DATE: ____________________

Directions: Put yourself into the story and describe *where* and *when* a part of the story takes place.

Where does the story take place?

Detail:	Detail:	Detail:

When does the story take place?

Detail:	Detail:	Detail:

STECK-VAUGHN IMPACT GRAPHIC NOVELS

Skill Master 6: **Cause and Effect**

NAME: ______________________ **DATE:** ______________________

Directions: Remember that causes are reasons. Effects are results. Follow the examples and fill in the blanks.

Cause	Effect
Cindy is worrying about her family's situation back home. She is not focused on doing well in the challenge.	**Example:** Some members of Team U.S.A. notice that something is wrong. Some of them get angry with Cindy for not having her head in the game.
Coach Wagner yells at his team to stop arguing when he enters a room and finds his teammates fighting. (p. 26)	
	Aisha goes for a jog around the streets of Moscow. (p. 30)
When a ground ball is hit to Maggie during the softball game, she can't decide whether to throw it home or to Ron at first base. (pp. 38–39)	
Dennis is searching the bleachers for his brother, Sammy, and he is one pitch away from striking out. Finally, he notices Sammy on Team U.S.A.'s bench. (p. 41)	

Lesson 4

Versus *Volume 4*
In Other Hands

Summary: Coach Wagner needs immediate surgery. Sammy has an emergency, too. Meanwhile, Ron's selfishness and Aisha's past threaten the team's success. Can they overcome these obstacles and defeat Team South Africa to advance to the next round in Tokyo?

Lesson Overview

Theme: Courage

Literary Response Skill: Foreshadowing

Comprehension Skill: Making Inferences

Literature Connection: *The Red Badge of Courage,* by Stephen Crane; *The Outsiders,* by S. E. Hinton

Before Reading

Set the Scene

Connect to Personal Experience

- Ask students to talk about a time when they had to be *courageous*—brave or emotionally strong—in the face of a problem.
- Have students give examples of famous people who battled illness or injury and came out on top.

Get Motivated

- Tell students that characters will face similar challenges in this volume.
- Distribute copies of *In Other Hands.* Turn to the inside front cover and point out the tips and strategies for reading graphic novels. Have students look at the cover, skim the pages, and share what they think will happen in this volume.

About the Characters

- Ask students to turn to pp. 2–3. Have a volunteer read the summary (p. 3). *Which characters can you relate to? Which character would you like to know better? Which members of Team U.S.A. will need the most courage to deal with their personal challenges?*

Focus on Literary Response: Foreshadowing

Teach

- Explain that writers sometimes provide hints or clues about events that will occur later in the plot. This is called *foreshadowing.* Have students turn back to pp. 2–3 of *In Other Hands.* Ask how the summary foreshadows either good or bad things.
- Read aloud Chapter 1, pp. 4–9. Model the following think-aloud: *Sammy thinks, "I have to keep Dennis's spirits up." He's hiding how sick he is. I wonder how long Sammy can keep his secret from Dennis. I wonder how Dennis will deal with it when he finds out.* (p. 9)

Read

- Pair students of differing abilities to read the rest of Chapter 1. Have partners read four pages silently, signal to the other with a thumbs-up or other silent signal when they're done, and wait quietly for the other to finish. Then each partner shares a thought about any clues they noticed that might foreshadow an important future event. Continue in this way to the end of the chapter.

Discuss

- Ask questions to help students understand foreshadowing:

  After reading page 13, how do you think Team U.S.A. will perform without Coach Wagner?

  Aisha decides to give in to Carla. Do you think Aisha will have enough courage to do the right thing in the end? (p. 18)

  As the others continue to ignore Ron, how do you think it will affect him and the team?

Write

- Distribute **Skill Master 7: Foreshadowing** on p. 24. Partners should read the examples of foreshadowing and make predictions about what will happen later in the story. Invite students to share their predictions.
- On a separate sheet of paper, ask students to predict what they think will happen to their favorite characters from *In Other Hands.* Have students explain the clues that help them make their predictions.

Skill Master 7

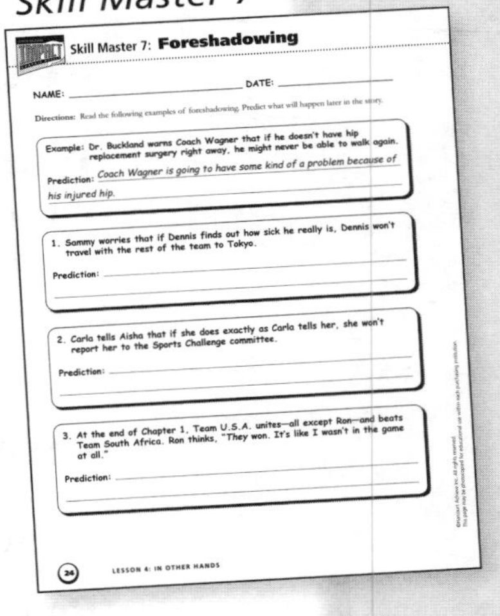
Skill Master 7: **Foreshadowing**

NAME: ______________________ DATE: ______________

Directions: Read the following examples of foreshadowing. Predict what will happen later in the story.

Example: Dr. Buckland warns Coach Wagner that if he doesn't have hip replacement surgery right away, he might never be able to walk again.

Prediction: *Coach Wagner is going to have some kind of a problem because of his injured hip.*

1. Sammy worries that if Dennis finds out how sick he really is, Dennis won't travel with the rest of the team to Tokyo.

Prediction: ______________________

2. Carla tells Aisha that if she does exactly as Carla tells her, she won't report her to the Sports Challenge committee.

Prediction: ______________________

3. At the end of Chapter 1, Team U.S.A. unites—all except Ron—and beats Team South Africa. Ron thinks, "They won. It's like I wasn't in the game at all."

Prediction: ______________________

24 LESSON 4: IN OTHER HANDS

ELL Support for English Language Learners

Help students become familiar with some of the idiomatic phrases used in Chapter 1: "I'll keep Dennis in check . . . " (p. 9); "I'll catch up with you at the hotel . . ." (p. 11); "Don't go soft on him . . ." (p. 16).

Focus on Comprehension: Making Inferences

Teach

- Explain that *inferences* are guesses one makes based on partial information. When an author doesn't say how someone feels, the reader can usually use clues—the tone of a character's voice, a narrowing of the eyes, whether she shouted, thought, or whispered something—to get a better idea of what's really happening.
- Describe a scene at an event such as a school dance. Ask students to make inferences on what people are wearing, the music, what will happen next, etc.

Support for Students with Special Needs

As an alternative to the writing activity, allow students to draw pictures of scenes in the story from which they made inferences. Students should indicate the clues in the scene they found helpful.

Skill Master 8

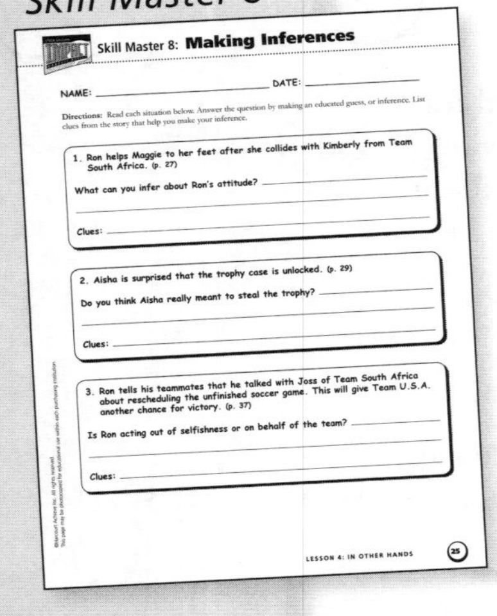
Skill Master 8: **Making Inferences**

NAME: ______ DATE: ______

Directions: Read each situation below. Answer the question by making an educated guess, or inference. List clues from the story that help you make your inference.

1. Ron helps Maggie to her feet after she collides with Kimberly from Team South Africa. (p. 27)

What can you infer about Ron's attitude? ______

Clues: ______

2. Aisha is surprised that the trophy case is unlocked. (p. 29)

Do you think Aisha really meant to steal the trophy? ______

Clues: ______

3. Ron tells his teammates that he talked with Joss of Team South Africa about rescheduling the unfinished soccer game. This will give Team U.S.A. another chance for victory. (p. 37)

Is Ron acting out of selfishness or on behalf of the team? ______

Clues: ______

©Harcourt Achieve Inc. All rights reserved. This page may be photocopied for educational use within each purchasing institution.

LESSON 4: IN OTHER HANDS 25

Read

- Have students summarize the events of Chapter 1. Pair students of differing abilities to read Chapter 2. Have partners read four pages silently, signal to the other with a thumbs-up or other silent signal when they're done, and wait quietly for the other to finish. Then each should share a thought about any inferences he or she made while reading. Continue in this way to the end of Chapter 2.

Discuss

- Guide students to understand how to make inferences in Chapter 2:

  What sacrifice is Dr. Buckland talking about when he speaks with Coach Wagner? (p. 24)

  What can you infer from Ron's actions when Maggie is hurt during the basketball game? (p. 27)

  Do you think Aisha will steal the trophy? Why? (p. 29)

  Do you think Team U.S.A. is going to win the game when the official tells Ron about the committee's rules? (p. 33)

Write

- Distribute **Skill Master 8: Making Inferences** on p. 25. Have student partners complete the activity. Invite volunteers to share.
- On a separate sheet of paper, ask students to describe an event without naming it. Invite volunteers to read their descriptions as their classmates try to name the event being described.

Review and Extend

Teach

- **Foreshadowing** Remind students that foreshadowing is the use of clues or hints to suggest events that will occur later in a story. Help students remember some of the foreshadowing used in *In Other Hands: What will Dennis do now that his brother is in the hospital? (p. 34) How will the rest of Team U.S.A. treat Ron after he gets their soccer match with Team South Africa rescheduled?*
- **Making Inferences** Remind students that making inferences is using clues in a story to make educated guesses about characters or events. Ask volunteers to describe inferences they made in Chapter 2.

Read

- Pair students of differing abilities to read Chapter 3. Have partners read four pages silently, signal to the other with a thumbs-up or other silent signal when they're done, and wait quietly for the other to finish. Then each student shares an example of foreshadowing or an inference they made while reading. Continue in this way to the end of the chapter.

Discuss

- Lead a discussion about foreshadowing and making inferences:

  What event foreshadows that Ron will make friends with the rest of Team U.S.A.? (p. 43)

  At the hospital, Cindy says to Aisha, "Shouldn't you be with him, too?" (p. 57) What can we infer from her comment?

  What event foreshadows that Ron will admit to Maggie that he was wrong? (p. 61)

Write

- Distribute copies of the **Writing Master** on p. 40. Ask students to write about one character who shows courage, including details from the story. Have students explain how courage helps the character reach his or her goals.

Writing Master

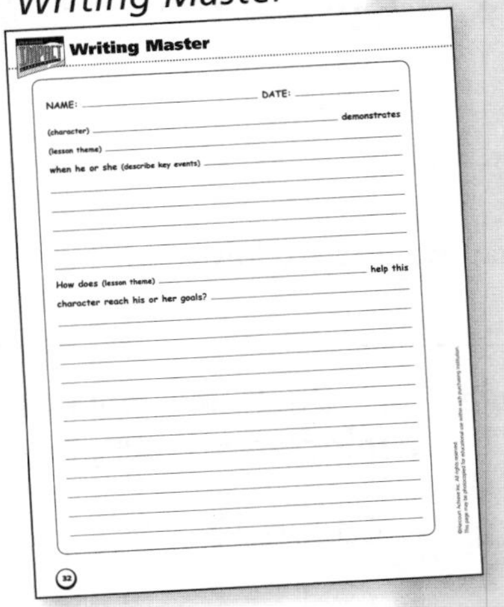
Writing Master

NAME: ____________ DATE: ____________

(character) ____________ demonstrates

(lesson theme) ____________

when he or she (describe key events) ____________

How does (lesson theme) ____________ help this

character reach his or her goals? ____________

After Reading

Wrap-Up

Discuss

- Allow students to reflect on what they have read.

  Which character would make a good best friend? Why?

  What do you think of Ron's attitude toward his teammates? How does he change? Why does he change?

  Which characters show good sportsmanship?

  What do you think Aisha should do about her secret?

  Have you ever faced a hard decision like the one Aisha has to make?

  Which character shows the most courage in In Other Hands*?*

Connect to Literature

Connect the theme of courage to other classroom literature, such as Stephen Crane's *The Red Badge of Courage* or S. E. Hinton's *The Outsiders.* For example:

- *In* The Red Badge of Courage, *Henry runs away when the enemy attacks a second time. When his regiment wins the battle, Henry feels ashamed and wishes he had been wounded like some of his fellow soldiers. A wound would be visible evidence of courage. Is there anyone in* In Other Hands *who wants to show courage but is too frightened? How is this situation different from what Henry goes through?*
- *When a church catches fire in* The Outsiders, *Ponyboy and Johnny rescue some children who are trapped inside. Ponyboy and Johnny show courage by endangering themselves to save the children. What characters in* In Other Hands *put the good of others ahead of themselves? What is the result of their actions?*

Skill Master 7: **Foreshadowing**

NAME: ______________________________ DATE: ____________________

Directions: Read the following examples of foreshadowing. Predict what will happen later in the story.

Example: Dr. Buckland warns Coach Wagner that if he doesn't have hip replacement surgery right away, he might never be able to walk again.

Prediction: *Coach Wagner is going to have some kind of a problem because of his injured hip.*

1. Sammy worries that if Dennis finds out how sick he really is, Dennis won't travel with the rest of the team to Tokyo.

   Prediction: ______________________________

   ____

2. Carla tells Aisha that if she does exactly as Carla tells her, she won't report her to the Sports Challenge committee.

   Prediction: ______________________________

   ____

3. At the end of Chapter 1, Team U.S.A. unites—all except Ron—and beats Team South Africa. Ron thinks, "*They* won. It's like I wasn't in the game at all."

   Prediction: ______________________________

   ____

TECK-VAUGHN IMPACT GRAPHIC NOVELS

Skill Master 8: **Making Inferences**

NAME: ______________________________ DATE: ____________________

Directions: Read each situation below. Answer the question by making an educated guess, or inference. List clues from the story that help you make your inference.

1. Ron helps Maggie to her feet after she collides with Kimberly from Team South Africa. (p. 27)

What can you infer about Ron's attitude? ______________________________

____

Clues: ____

2. Aisha is surprised that the trophy case is unlocked. (p. 29)

Do you think Aisha really meant to steal the trophy? ____________________

____

Clues: ____

3. Ron tells his teammates that he talked with Joss of Team South Africa about rescheduling the unfinished soccer game. This will give Team U.S.A. another chance for victory. (p. 37)

Is Ron acting out of selfishness or on behalf of the team? ____________________

____

Clues: ____

Lesson 5

Versus *Volume 5*
To the Wire

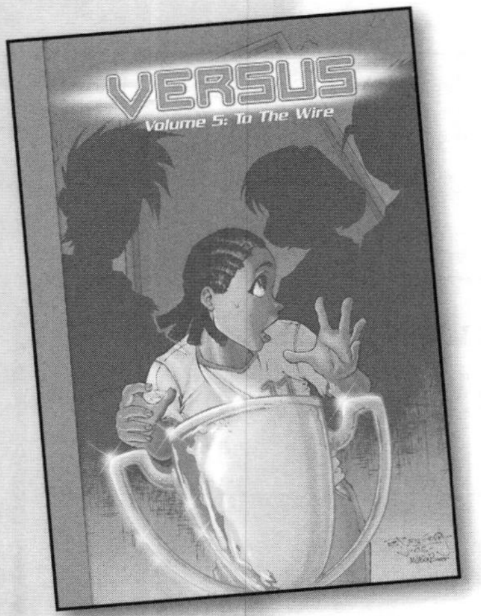

Summary: Team U.S.A. travels to Japan for their final competition. They discover an unlikely new leader—Ron. Dennis feels guilty about competing while Sammy recovers from brain surgery. Aisha steals the trophy, but can she still hide her secret? Will Team U.S.A. pull together and win it all?

Lesson Overview

Theme: Responsibility

Literary Response Skill: Analyze Irony

Comprehension Skill: Identifying Theme

Literature Connection: *The Call of the Wild,* by Jack London; *The Pigman,* by Paul Zindel

Before Reading

Set the Scene

Connect to Personal Experience

- Ask students to describe a recent time when they were trusted with something important or had to show good judgment. Have they ever had to take care of younger siblings or be in charge of someone else's money? Was it difficult? What might have happened had they not shown good judgment?
- Have students give examples of jobs in which people are *responsible* for, or trusted with, other people's lives or safety. Ask them to explain how bad judgment in these jobs could affect others.

Get Motivated

- Tell students that the book will conclude the story of Team U.S.A. Coach Jerry and the players are faced with challenges that test their responsibility to themselves and the team.
- Distribute copies of *To the Wire.* Turn to the inside front cover and review the instructions for reading graphic novels. Have students look at the cover, skim the pages, and share what they think is going to happen.

About the Characters

- Ask students to turn to pp. 2–3. Have a volunteer read the summary (p. 3). *Do you think Team U.S.A. will overcome its obstacles and win the competition? Which players do you think will face the most challenges?*

During Reading

Focus on Literary Response: Analyze Irony

Teach

- Explain that *irony* is the difference between what is expected and what really happens. Offer examples of irony in everday life to help students understand the concept: *Have you ever been called into the principal's office? What's the first thing you think of? Instead of getting in trouble, imagine the principal gives you a special award for good citizenship. You leave the office relieved and feeling great. You didn't expect that at all.*
- Read aloud Chapter 1, pp. 4–9. Model the following think-aloud: *On page 5, we think Aisha steals the trophy. On page 6, we realize she doesn't. Irony makes the story more interesting because now we wonder what the criminals will do to Aisha.*

Read

- Pair students of differing abilities to read the rest of Chapter 1. Have partners read four pages silently, signal to the other with a thumbs-up or other silent signal when they're done, and wait quietly for the other to finish. Partners should share any ironies they discover. Continue in this way to the end of the chapter.

Discuss

- Ask questions to help students gain an understanding of irony:

  Dennis is torn between staying with Sammy and being a responsible teammate. (p. 8) What do we expect him to do?

  What is ironic about Ron showing the highlight video? (p. 12)

  During the soccer match, Aisha spots the criminals in the crowd. (p. 21) What's ironic about the signs they're holding?

Write

- Distribute **Skill Master 9: Irony** on p. 30. Students can work with their partners to complete the activity. Have students read the sample sentences and then complete the chart. Ask volunteers to share their sentences.
- Ask students to think about their favorite book, movie, or TV show. On a seperate sheet of paper, have them write about how the plot or a character demonstrates irony by turning out differently than expected.

ELL Support for English Language Learners

Point out examples of slang or idiomatic phrases from Chapter 1 of *To the Wire:* "slime bag" (p. 4); "weak in the knees" (p. 5); "Sherlock Holmes" (p. 7); "jumping at shadows" (p. 7); "loosen up" (p. 13); "get settled" (p. 15); "bend the rules" (p. 17). Ask volunteers to explain their meanings.

Skill Master 9

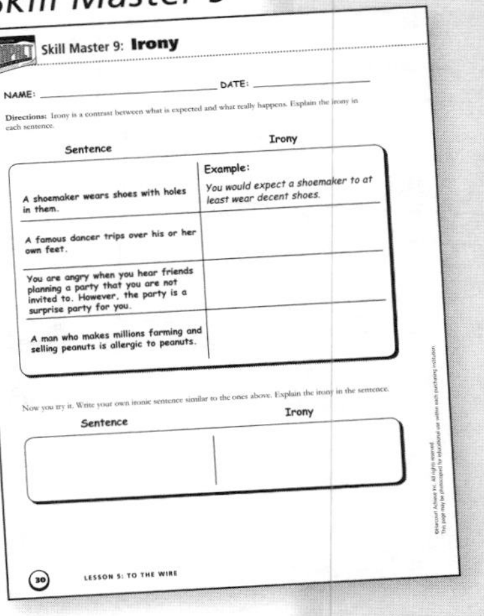
Skill Master 9: **Irony**

NAME: ______ DATE: ______

Directions: Irony is a contrast between what is expected and what really happens. Explain the irony in each sentence.

Sentence	Irony
A shoemaker wears shoes with holes in them.	Example: *You would expect a shoemaker to at least wear decent shoes.*
A famous dancer trips over his or her own feet.	
You are angry when you hear friends planning a party that you are not invited to. However, the party is a surprise party for you.	
A man who makes millions farming and selling peanuts is allergic to peanuts.	

Now you try it. Write your own ironic sentence similar to the ones above. Explain the irony in the sentence.

Sentence	Irony

30 LESSON 5: TO THE WIRE

Focus on Comprehension: Identifying Theme

Teach

- Explain that authors frequently suggest an important idea or life lesson in their writing. This is called a *theme.* A theme isn't exactly the same as the moral of a story, but it's similar. A theme usually isn't openly stated. Instead, the reader must think about the elements of the story and make an inference, or educated guess, about the important idea that is being suggested.
- Recount the plot of a familiar story or movie. Include important details about the plot and the characters' actions. Ask volunteers to suggest the theme of the story or movie. For example: *Star Wars* (good overcomes evil), *The Miracle Worker* (perseverance).

Support for **Students with Special Needs**

During the discussion of Chapter 2, expand on the questions to allow students to investigate each one more thoroughly. For example, for the question *How does Dennis feel about leaving his brother behind?* (p. 26), lead students by asking: *Why does Dennis feel guilty? Why did he want to stay with Sammy?*

Skill Master 10

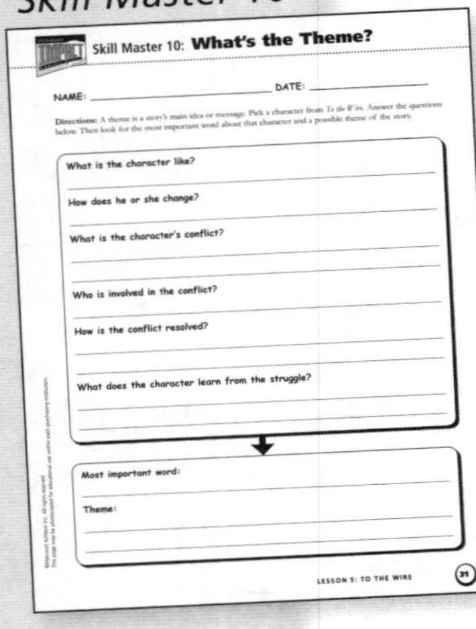
Skill Master 10: **What's the Theme?**

NAME: ______________________ DATE: ______________

Directions: A theme is a story's main idea or message. Pick a character from *To the Wire*. Answer the questions below. Then look for the most important word about that character and a possible theme of the story.

What is the character like?

How does he or she change?

What is the character's conflict?

Who is involved in the conflict?

How is the conflict resolved?

What does the character learn from the struggle?

Most important word:

Theme:

LESSON 5: TO THE WIRE 31

Read

- Pair students of differing abilities to read Chapter 2, urging students to look for important details that might suggest the story's theme. Have partners read four pages silently, signal to the other with a thumbs-up or other silent signal when they're done, and wait quietly for the other to finish. Partners should share thoughts about the theme. Continue in this way to the end of the chapter.

Discuss

- Ask questions to help students find possible themes in Chapter 2:

  How does Dennis feel about leaving Sammy behind? Why does Dennis feel responsible for taking care of Sammy? (p. 26)

  When Aisha steals the trophy (p. 33), do you think she does the right thing? Is it a responsible decision?

  On page 42, what attitude does Ron display? Why does he take responsibility for supporting the team?

  Based on the actions of Dennis and Aisha, name one theme suggested in Chapter 2. (It's still possible for troubled people to offer support to others.)

Write

- Distribute **Skill Master 10: What's the Theme?** on p. 31. Have partners complete the activity. Ask volunteers to share their results. Multiple themes may be suggested.

- Ask students to think about their favorite characters from *To the Wire*. On a separate sheet of paper, have them list possible themes associated with the character's behavior or attitude.

Review and Extend

Teach

- **Analyze Irony** Remind students that irony is the difference between what is expected and what actually happens. For example: *You look out the window on a bright, sunny day and walk outside to find freezing temperatures.*

- **Identifying Theme** Remind students that the theme is the important idea suggested in a story. The theme is not usually stated. Instead, readers must make inferences about the important idea the author wants to share. Ask a volunteer to choose a character and recall what happens to this person in Chapter 2. Have other students assist in finding how the character's experiences suggest a theme.

Read

- Pair students of differing abilities to read Chapter 3. Remind students to think about themes, paying attention to how characters change and grow. Have partners read four pages silently, signal to the other with a thumbs-up or other silent signal when they're done, and wait quietly for the other to finish. Partners should share observations about irony or theme. Continue in this way to the end of Chapter 3.

Discuss

- Lead students in a discussion about examples of irony in *To the Wire*. Also, lead them into a better understanding of the theme:

  How does Aisha surprise the criminals when she steals the trophy? (pp. 47–48) What is ironic about Coach Wagner and Aisha's secret? (p. 56)

  How does Ron go from thinking he's better than everyone to being a team player? What does he learn? How does his change suggest one theme for the story? (A team of 12 people is stronger than 12 separate individuals.)

  What effect does Dennis's sense of responsibility have on his actions? What theme does the brothers' relationship suggest?

Write

- Distribute copies of the **Writing Master** on p. 40. Ask students to choose one character from the story and describe key events showing that character demonstrating responsibility. Ask students to tell how the character's traits help or hinder the character in reaching his or her goals.

Writing Master

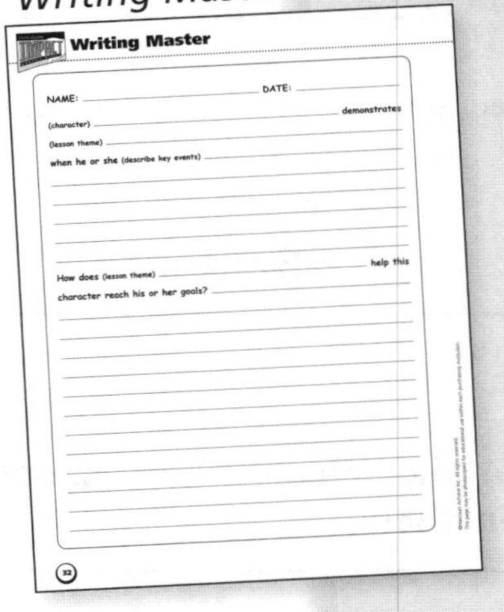
Writing Master

NAME: DATE:

(character) demonstrates

(lesson theme)

when he or she (describe key events)

How does (lesson theme) help this

character reach his or her goals?

32

After Reading

Wrap-Up

Discuss

- Allow students to reflect on what they have read.

  How do some of the characters change to make the team stronger?

  Which character changes the most? Why do you think so?

  Which of the characters' actions surprise or disappoint you?

  Which character started out as your favorite? Did this change as you read more?

  What would you have done if you were Aisha?

Connect to Literature

Connect the theme of responsibility to other classroom literature, such as London's *The Call of the Wild* or Zindel's *The Pigman*. For example:

- *Buck, a dog in* The Call of the Wild, *is torn between living free in the wilderness or remaining in the world of men. Buck shows responsibility among men by caring for the other members of the sled team and in the wild by being a dominant but caring leader of the wolf pack. What characters in* To the Wire *show responsibility? How are the situations in the two books alike? How are they different?*
- *In* The Pigman, *John and Lorraine enjoy spending time with Angelo Pignati, whom they call the Pigman, but they take advantage of him and bear some responsibility for his death. Which characters in* To the Wire *use people to get what they want? How are John and Lorraine different from the characters in* To the Wire?

Skill Master 9: **Irony**

NAME: ______________________________ DATE: ____________________

Directions: Irony is a contrast between what is expected and what really happens. Explain the irony in each sentence.

Sentence	Irony
A shoemaker wears shoes with holes in them.	**Example:** *You would expect a shoemaker to at least wear decent shoes.*
A famous dancer trips over his or her own feet.	
You are angry when you hear friends planning a party that you are not invited to. However, the party is a surprise party for you.	
A man who makes millions farming and selling peanuts is allergic to peanuts.	

Now you try it. Write your own ironic sentence similar to the ones above. Explain the irony in the sentence.

Sentence	Irony